BLUEBERRIES
FARMING

The beginner's guide to growing blueberries from varieties to harvesting

Davies Cheruiyot

BLUEBERRIES FARMING

CONTENTS

ACKNOWLEDGMENTS

I would like to express my gratitude to many people who saw me through the book; to all those who provided support, talked things over, read, wrote, offered comments, allowed me to
quote their remarks and assisted in editing, proofreading and design

1 INTRODUCTION TO BLUEBERRIES FARMING

Introduction to Blueberries farming

Blueberries are shrubs which are deciduous. Their leaves are elliptical with stems that are dotted. They produce flowers that range from white to pink. their seeds are small in size. blueberries are believed to have originated i North America but have now spread to most parts of the world. Blueberries are rich in Vitamin c, fiber, Manganese and Vitamin K among other mineral components.

Blueberries come from the family of Ericaceae and the genus of Vaccinium.

Benefits of Blueberries

1. Blueberries contain the necessary nutritional requirements required for proper functioning of the body like Vitamin C, Vitamin K, Manganese and fiber.
2. Blueberries may help in improving the health of the skin because of Vitamin Content available in them.
3. Blueberries may help in digestion because of the high fiber content available in the fruits
4. Blueberries may help in improving heart condition
5. Blueberries may help in lowering blood pressure
6. Blueberries may help in prevention of diabetes.

2 BLUEBERRIES VARIETIES

VARIETIES

Blueberries can be categorized into the following categories;

1.   Northern highbush
2.   Southern highbush
3.   Low bush
4.   Rabbiteye
5.   Half-high

1.   Northern highbush

Northern Highbush blueberries belong to hardy types and can grow up to 8 feet when they mature.

2.   Southern Highbush

Southern Highbush are not as hardy like Northern Highbush category types and they can grow to 7 inches when they are mature.

3.   low bush

low bush are also referred to as wild berries. They grow to I feet when they are mature just as the name suggests.

4.   Rabbiteye

Rabbiteye grow up to 8 feet when they are mature although they are not adaptive to cooler climatic conditions.

5.   Half-high

Half-high are hybrid just as the name suggests. Half-High came as a result of crossing low bush and highbush blueberries. They grow to 4 inches when they are mature.

Varieties.

The following are the most common blueberry varieties;

• Northern Highbush varieties

These blueberry varieties are adaptive to harsh and cold conditions. They can grow to 7 feet when they are mature

The following are the most common Northern Highbush varieties;

1. Duke
2. Earl blue
3. Pink Lemonade
4. Sweetheart
5. Patriot

1.   Duke

Duke blueberries were first developed in Maryland in the 1987's.

Characteristics

- They thrive well in zones 4 to 7
- They are adaptive to most climatic conditions
- They grow to 6 feet tall when mature
- Their flowers are white in color
- Their fruits are large in size

2.   Earl blue

Earl blue originated in the 1952's

Characteristics

- They thrive well in zones 5 to 7
- Their flowers are white to pink in color
- They grow to 6 feet tall when mature
- Their fruits are medium to large in size

3. Pink Lemonade

Pink Lemonade blueberries were developed in the 1996's

Characteristics

- They thrive well in zones 4-8
- They are resistant to cold climatic conditions
- Their flowers are pink in color
- Their fruits are medium in size

4.   Sweetheart

Sweetheart blueberries were developed in 2010.

Characteristics

- They thrive well in zones 4-8
- They grow to 6 feet tall when mature
- Their flowers are white in color
- Their fruits are large in size

5.   Patriot

Patriot blueberries were developed in the 1976's

Characteristics

- They thrive well in zones 3-7
- They are resistant to most climatic conditions
- Their flowers are white and pink in color
- They grow to 5 feet tall when mature
- Their fruits are large In size

• Southern Highbush varieties

Most of Southern Highbush varieties can grow to 6 feet tall. The most common southern Highbush varieties are;

1. Jubilee
2. Jewel
3. O'Neal
4. Misty
5. Sunshine

1. Jubilee

Jubilee blueberries were developed in the 1994's

Characteristics

- They thrive well in zones 5-9
- They are resistant to heat conditions
- They grow to 6 feet tall when mature
- Their flowers are pink and white in color
- Their fruits have powdery blue colors
- Their fruits are medium in size

2. Jewel

Characteristics

- They thrive well in zones 6-9
- They grow to 4 feet when mature
- They are resistant to hot conditions
- Their fruits are large in size

3. O'Neal blueberries

O'Neal blueberries were developed in the 1987's

Characteristics

- They thrive well in zones 5-9
- They grow to 6 feet tall when mature
- They are resistant to hot climatic conditions
- Their flowers are white and pink in color
- Their fruits are large in size

4. Misty

Misty blueberries were developed in the 1989's

Characteristics

- They thrive well inn zones 6-10
- They are resistant to hot climatic conditions
- Their flowers are pink in color
- Their fruits are medium to large in size

5.   Sunshine

Sunshine blueberries were developed in the 1979's

Characteristics

- They thrive well in zones 5-10
- They grow to 4 feet tall when mature
- Their flowers are white and pink in color
- Their fruits are medium in size

• **Low bush varieties**

Low bush blueberries are also referred to a wild blueberries. Most of the varieties grow to 2 feet tall. The most common Low bush blueberries are;

1. Dwarf Tophat
2. Velvetleaf
3. Brunswick
4. Bushel and Berry Blueberry Buckle

1.   Dwarf Tophat

Dwarf Tophat are perfect for indoor growing.

Characteristics

- They thrive well in zones 3-7
- Their flowers are white in color
- They grow to 2 feet tall when mature
- Their fruits have dusky blue colors
- Their fruits are large in size

2. Velvetleaf

Velvetleaf are also referred to as Canadian blueberries.

Characteristics

- They thrive well in zone s4-8
- They grow to 2 feet tall when mature
- Their fruits are blue in color
- Their fruits are large in size

3.   Brunswick

Characteristics

- They thrive well in zones 3-8
- They grow to 2 feet when mature
- Their flowers are white in color
- Their fruits are blue in color
- Their fruits are medium in size

4. Bushel and Berry blueberry buckle

These blueberries are good for indoor growing

Characteristics

- They thrive well in zone s 6-10
- They grow to 2 feet when mature
- Their flowers are large in color
- Their fruits are large in color
- Their fruits are blue in color

- ## **Rabbteyee blueberries**

Most Rabbiteye blueberries can grow up to 8 feet tall. The most common Rabbiteye blueberries are;

1. Vernon
2. Premier
3. Brightwell
4. Ocklockonee
5. Desoto

1.   Vernon

Vernon blueberries produces their fruits early.

Characteristics

- They thrive well in zones 6-9
- Their produce a lot of fruits
- Their fruits are large in size
- Their fruits are blue in color

2.   Premier

Characteristics
- They thrive well in zones 6-9

- Their trees are produce more fruits
- They grow to 7 feet when mature
- Their fruits are blue and large in size

3.   Brightwell

Characteristics

- They thrive well in zones 7-9
- They grow to 7 feet when mature
- They produce lots of fruits
- Their fruits are blue and medium in size

4.   Ochlocknee

Characteristics

- They thrive well in zones 6-9
- They grow to 6 feet tall when mature
- Their fruits are blue and large in size
- Their flowers bloom late

5. Desoto

Characteristics

- They thrive well in zones 6-9
- They grow to 6 feet tall when mature
- Their flowers bloom late
- Their fruits are blue and large in color

• Half-High blueberries

Half -High blueberries came as a result of crossing low bush and Northern Highbush blueberries. Most of their varieties grow up to 4 feet tall. The most common Half-High blueberries are;

1. Chippewa
2. Bushel and Berry Jelly Bean
3. Dwarf North blue
4. Dwarf Northsky
5. Northvountry

1. Chippewa

Characteristics

- They thrive well in zones 3-7
- They are resistant to most climatic conditions
- They grow to 4 feet tall when mature
- Their fruits produce blue and large fruits.

2. Bushel and Berry Jelly Bean

Characteristics

- They thrive well in zones 4-8
- They are resistant to most climatic conditions
- They grow to 2 feet when mature
- Their flowers bloom late
- Their fruits are blue and large In size

3.   Dwarf North blue

Characteristics

- They are great for container growing
- They thrive well in zones 3-7
- They grow to 2 feet when mature
- Their flowers bloom in mid Summer

4.   Dwarf Northsky

Characteristics

- They thrive well in zones 3-7
- They grow to 2 feet tall when mature
- Their flowers bloom in mid spring
- Their fruits are large in size and blue in color

5.   North country blueberries

Characteristics

BLUEBERRIES FARMING

- They thrive well in zones 3-7
- They are resistant to cold climatic conditions
- Their flowers are large in color
- Their fruits are medium in size and blue in color
- They grow to 3 feet tall when mature

3 BLUEBERRIES GROWING REQUIREMENTS

BLUEBERRIES GROWING REQUIREMENTS

Climatic conditions

Blueberries should be planted in a place that has accessible sunlight with some shelter to protect them from excessive wind.

Container growing of blueberries

blueberries can be grown in containers. The varieties that can be planted in containers are; Pink Lemonade, Pink Champagne and Top Hat. The containers to be used should be large in size. Ensure that the holes have drainage. Buy potting mix that has compost, peat moss and sand soils then plant the bush in the prepared potting mix. Ensure that you water them frequently. Mulching can be done to the blueberry plants so that the moisture content is preserved.

Soil requirements

The soils that blueberries are to be planted on should be acidic with P.H range of 4 to 5. Acidity levels can be achieved by adding peat moss, pine bark or granulated Sulphur to the soils.

 The soils should be able to hold moisture because blueberries have roots that are shallow.

Planting

Plant blueberries in spring or late fall. When planting blueberries you should ensure that the root ball is below the surface because planting them deep will make them to find it hard growing. Holes should be dug about 18 inches in depth and 17 inches in width. Bushes should be spaced 5 feet apart in rows and the distance between the rows should be 7 feet. Once that is done, you should prepare organic mixture of peat moss, compost, 2 parts of oak leaf and 3 parts of loam to the bottom of the dug hole. Then place the root ball below the surface. Ensure that the roots are spread out, then refill the soils lightly. After 4 weeks apply 10-10-10 fertilizer

Mulching

Ensure that you mulch your blueberry plants to about 3 inches of mulch. This is necessary so that the moisture content is preserved, weeds are prevented and organic matter is added to the soils.

Care

The following are the management practices for better blueberries;

- Apply 10-10-10 fertilizer annually for your blueberry plants
- Prune the blueberry plants the first two years so that when fruit bearing stage begins the production rates will increase.
- Water blueberry plants at least twice a week
- Mulch blueberry plants so that the moisture content is preserved thus allowing the flowering stage to happen at the right time thus more fruits.

Pruning

Pruning should be done in early spring or late winter before the beginning of new growths.

Broken, dead and shoots that are spindling should be pruned. Cut all the stems for low bush blueberries at the ground level. Remove woods for highbush varieties especially those that are more than 5 years old specifically those that are crowded. Spindly twigs should also be removed.

4 BLUEBERRIES PESTS AND DISEASES

BLUEBERRIES PESTS AND DSEASES

The following are the most common blueberry pests and diseases;

1. Anthracnose
2. Black Canker
3. Root Rot
4. Alternaria Blight
5. Blueberry Gall Midges
6. Blueberry Seed Weevils
7. Mealybugs
8. Blueberry Scales

1.   Anthracnose

Anthracnose is a fungal disease which is usually noticeable during humid conditions and is common during fruit set stage and flowering stages. They affect blueberry leaves, flowers and fruits.

Symptoms

- Black spots on blueberry lesions
- Blueberry young shoots defoliation
- Spots which are small and black on blueberry flowers
- Sunken spots on blueberry fruits

Prevention

- Infected leaves and fruits should be removed and destroyed
- Blueberry fruits should be stored in a cool and dry place.

2.   Black canker

Black leg is a fungal disease which is seed borne and is spread through infested seedlings or planting materials that have been infested.

Symptoms

- Light brown spots on blueberry leaves
- Dark cankers on blueberry stems
- Weak blueberry root systems
- Wilting of blueberry plants
- Dying of blueberry plants

Prevention

- Ensure that blueberry seeds are from a certified source and are free from diseases and pests
- Ensure that the soils are properly drained
- Ensure that blueberry orchard is free from weeds

3.   Root Rot

Blueberry root Rot is a fungal disease which affects the root especially in soils that are not well drained.

Symptoms

- Improper blueberry fruit formation
- Wilting of blueberry leaves
- Dying of blueberry leaves
- Decaying of trees

Prevention

- Affected blueberry trees should be uprooted
- Ensure that the soils are well drained

4.   Alternaria blight

Altenaria blight is a disease which affects the fruits and leaves of blueberries.

Symptoms

- leaf spots on blueberry leaves
- concentric rings on blueberry leaves
- dropping of blueberry leaves

prevention

- ensure that the blueberry orchard is always clean
- ensure that the blueberry seeds are from a certified source and are free from pests and diseases

5.   Blueberry Gall midges

Blueberry Gall Midge are insects which are small in size with about 2 mm in length. their larvae mine the leaves of blueberry plants .

Symptoms

- Galls on blueberry leaves
- Circular galls on the leaf surface
- Wrinkling of blueberry leaves
- Dropping of blueberry leaves

Prevention

- Ensure that the blueberry orchard is free from weeds
- crowded blueberry branches should be pruned

6.   Blueberries seed weevils

Blueberries seed weevil are insects which are brown grayish in color and are usually active after dusk. They feed on flower buds and leaves of blueberry plants.

Symptoms

- Dropping of flowers
- Dropping of leaves

Prevention

- Infected blueberry leaves and flowers should be removed and destroyed.

7.   mealybugs

mealybugs suck the sap of blueberry leaves and fruits.

Symptoms

- yellowish color on blueberry leaves
- drying of blueberry leaves
- sooty molds
  prevention
- Infested leaves should be removed and destroyed
- Practice weed management practices

8.   Blueberry Scales

Blueberry scales are insects which are red to white, round and small in size. They suck the cell sap of the blueberry plants.

Symptoms

- Pale green to yellowish color on infested blueberry leaves
- Dying of blueberry leaves
- Dropping of blueberry leaves
- Stunted growth rates
- Dying of blueberry branches
- Sooty molds

Prevention

- Infested leaves should be removed and destroyed

5 HARVESTING AND POST-HARVESTING

HARVESTING AND POST-HARVESTING

Harvesting

Blueberries mature between June and august depending on the variety planted usually between 60 to 95 days. Blueberries that are ripe will have dark blue colors, can easily be removed and will have excellent flavors. Blueberries can yield an average of 6 kgs of berries. Blueberries ripen faster during hot conditions unlike during cold conditions. A blueberry picker can be used for picking blueberries and placed in bowls.

Post-harvesting

Storing

Blueberries can be stored between 0 degrees Celsius to 2 degrees Celsius and high humidity of 91 to 95 percent for around 14 days before they begin to soften.

Preservation

Blueberries are used in making juices, freezing, boiling and in production of jam. Blueberries should be freeze immediately after harvesting.

ABOUT THE AUTHOR

Davies Cheruiyot is an agribusiness specialist with a degree in agribusiness. He turned to farming in 2015 to expand his knowledge on agriculture. He is the author of Pineapple farming, Mango farming, Strawberry farming and several other books

Made in the USA
Coppell, TX
01 July 2023

18677200R00036